Insights of the
Psalms

Insights of the
Psalms

Written and compiled by
Andrea Skevington

LION

Text copyright © 2006 Andrea Skevington
This edition copyright © 2006 Lion Hudson

The author asserts the moral right
to be identified as the author of this work

A Lion Book
an imprint of
Lion Hudson plc
Mayfield House, 256 Banbury Road,
Oxford OX2 7DH, England
www.lionhudson.com
ISBN-13: 978-0-7459-5217-8
ISBN-10: 0-7459-5217-8

First edition 2006
10 9 8 7 6 5 4 3 2 1 0

Picture acknowledgments

pp. 15, 20, 26, 33, 38, 44 copyright ©
Alamy Ltd; pp. 8–9, 11, 36, 46–47
copyright © Digital Vision; p. 6 copyright
© Bill Bain.

Text acknowledgments

pp. 8, 10, 13, 19, 25, 28, 30, 31, 34, 36,
38, 40, 42 and 48 are Scripture
quotations taken from the Holy Bible,
New International Version, copyright ©
1973, 1978, 1984 International Bible
Society. Used by permission of
Zondervan and Hodder and Stoughton
Limited. All rights reserved.

pp. 14, 22-23, 26, 33, 35, 44 and 45 are
Scripture quotations taken from the Holy
Bible, English Standard Version,
published by Harper Collins Publishers,
copyright © 2001 Crossway Bibles, a
division of Good News Publishers. Used
by permission. All rights reserved.

p. 9 is a Scripture quotation taken from
the Holy Bible, New Living Translation,
copyright © 1996. Used by permission
of Tyndale House Publishers, Inc.,
Wheaton, Illinois 60189. All rights
reserved.

pp. 12, 16–17, 21, 29 and 42-43 are
Scripture quotations taken from The New
American Standard Bible, copyright ©
1960, 1962, 1963, 1968, 1971, 1972,
1973, 1975, 1977, 1995 by The
Lockman Foundation. Used by
permission.

pp. 17–18, 24, 37 and 41 are Scripture
quotations taken from taken from the
Contemporary English Version, copyright
© 1995 by American Bible Society. Used
by permission.

pp. 15 and 16 are Scripture quotations
taken from from the Authorized Version
of the Bible (King James Bible), the rights
in which are vested in the Crown, are
reproduced by permission of the
Crown's Patentee, Cambridge University
Press.

A catalogue record for this book is
available from the British Library

Typeset in Helvetica Neue Light

Printed and bound in China

Contents

Introduction

The psalms are a truly remarkable collection of poems and songs. They are deeply personal, and yet are spoken and sung by congregations in churches everywhere. They are often written to an individual's precise circumstances, but they echo through the ages and into our own lives. Jesus quoted from them often.

The psalms do not shy away from difficulties and dangers. They speak of anger and vengeance, and the pain of sin and guilt. They are passionate about justice, and among them are nature poems which open the eyes of many to the spiritual power of the wilderness.

Above all, these are poems written by real, fallible human beings. And here is their greatest strength. When we read them, we are aware that whatever emotions we may find ourselves experiencing – joy or despair – we are not alone. Others share the same human condition, and have found a way of bringing their lives, their hopes and their fears to God.

As you read, you may be moved to make some of these prayers and poems personal to you.

God the Creator

The earth is the Lord's, and everything in it,
the world, and all who live in it;
for he founded it upon the seas
and established it upon the waters.
Psalm 24:1–2

When I look at the night sky

We can imagine King David, alone in the desert, overawed at the beauty of the night sky. Such beauty can turn our thoughts to God, and to the power and energy of his creation. Acknowledging that everything is God's workmanship can also remind us of our responsibility to care for this extraordinary world.

O Lord, our Lord, the majesty of your name
   fills the earth!
Your glory is higher than the heavens.
You have taught children and nursing infants
to give you praise.
They silence your enemies
who were seeking revenge.
When I look at the night sky
and see the work of your fingers –
the moon and the stars you have set in place –
what are mortals that you should think of us,
mere humans that you should care for us?
For you made us only a little lower than God,
and you crowned us with glory and honour.
You put us in charge of everything you made,
giving us authority over all things –
the sheep and the cattle
and all the wild animals,
the birds in the sky, the fish in the sea,
and everything that swims the ocean currents.
O Lord, our Lord, the majesty of your name
   fills the earth!

Psalm 8

The skies pour out speech

Nature has the power to tell us of God's character – it is a living parable of the creator. This parable can speak to all people at all times, making it precious indeed. Meditating on these words of vigour and strength will help us to see the power and beauty of God.

The heavens declare the glory of God;
the skies proclaim the work of his hands.
Day after day they pour forth speech;
night after night they display knowledge.
There is no speech or language
where their voice is not heard.
Their voice goes out into all the earth,
their words to the ends of the world.
In the heavens he has pitched a tent for the sun,
which is like a bridegroom coming forth from his pavilion,
like a champion rejoicing to run his course.
It rises at one end of the heavens
and makes its circuit to the other;
nothing is hidden from its heat.
Psalm 19:1–6

The trees of the Lord drink their fill

It is awe-inspiring to think of God inhabiting his creation – robed in light, living in the tent of the heavens. Perhaps when we think of it we can get a glimpse of him constantly at work; his creative energies sustaining and renewing the wilderness, the field and us alike. And we are reminded of our dependence on God, providing a powerful antidote to a modern, urban detachment from nature.

Bless the Lord, O my soul!
O Lord my God, you are very great;
You are clothed with splendour and majesty,
Covering yourself with light as with a cloak,
Stretching out heaven like a tent curtain.
He waters the mountains from his upper chambers;
The earth is satisfied with the fruit of his works.
He causes the grass to grow for the cattle,
And vegetation for the labour of man,
So that he may bring forth food from the earth,
And wine which makes man's heart glad,
So that he may make his face glisten with oil,
And food which sustains man's heart.
The trees of the Lord drink their fill,
The cedars of Lebanon which he planted,
Where the birds build their nests,
And the stork, whose home is the fir trees.
You open your hand, they are satisfied with good.
Psalm 104:1–2, 13–17, 28

God Our Help and Guide

He turned the desert into pools of water
and the parched ground into flowing springs;
there he brought the hungry to live,
and they founded a city where they could settle.
Psalm 107:35–36

My help comes from God

Sometimes, we can only call for help silently – by raising our eyes, or our hands. And God's loving response to our silence helps us to lay aside thoughts of trouble, and dwell instead on the loving actions of a God whose care is gentle and constant.

I lift up my eyes to the hills.
From where does my help come?
My help comes from the Lord,

who made heaven and earth.
He will not let your foot be moved;
he who keeps you will not slumber.
Behold, he who keeps Israel
will neither slumber nor sleep.
The Lord is your keeper;
the Lord is your shade on your right hand.
The sun shall not strike you by day,
nor the moon by night.
The Lord will keep you from all evil;
he will keep your life.
The Lord will keep
your going out and your coming in
from this time forth and forevermore.
Psalm 121

Guided by a loving hand

In Psalm 23, possibly the most well-loved of all the psalms, we see God leading David as a shepherd leads a sheep. A shepherd's concern is for the welfare of his sheep – wanting only what is best for them. So it is with God. Sometimes, we can be so busy and preoccupied that we do not notice the green pastures and still waters in our lives. David's words can encourage us to open our eyes and see them.

The Lord is my shepherd; I shall not want.
He maketh me to lie down in green pastures:
he leadeth me beside the still waters.
He restoreth my soul: he leadeth me in the paths of
righteousness for his name's sake.
Yea, though I walk through the valley of the shadow of
death, I will fear no evil: for thou art with me; thy rod and
thy staff they comfort me.

*Thou preparest a table before me in the presence of
mine enemies: thou anointest my head with oil;
    my cup runneth over.
Surely goodness and mercy shall follow me all the
days of my life: and I will dwell in the house of the
Lord for ever.*
Psalm 23

The one who is always ready to help

This next psalm contrasts the powerful of this world
with God. These rulers, who appear so invincible and
so great, will not last. But God, who made the earth,
does last. He is on the side of the oppressed, the
hungry and the bowed down, and those who seek
what is right.

*Do not trust in princes,
In mortal man, in whom there is no salvation.
His spirit departs, he returns to the earth;
In that very day his thoughts perish.
How blessed is he whose help is the God of Jacob,
Whose hope is in the Lord his God,
Who made heaven and earth,
The sea and all that is in them;
Who keeps faith forever;
Who executes justice for the oppressed;*

Who gives food to the hungry?
The Lord sets the prisoners free.
The Lord opens the eyes of the blind;
The Lord raises up those who are bowed down;
The Lord loves the righteous;
The Lord protects the strangers;
He supports the fatherless and the widow,
But he thwarts the way of the wicked.
Psalm 146:3–9

The way to happiness

This psalm shows how God can feed and nurture us,
and how following his ways can bring us a fruitful life
of peace.

God blesses those people
who refuse evil advice
and won't follow sinners
or join in sneering at God.
Instead, the Law of the Lord
makes them happy,
and they think about it
day and night.

They are like trees
growing beside a stream,
trees that produce
fruit in season
and always have leaves.
Those people succeed
in everything they do.
Psalm 1:1–3

God Who Forgives

Set a guard over my mouth, O Lord;
keep watch over the door of my lips.
Let not my heart be drawn to what is evil,
to take part in wicked deeds.
Psalm 141:3–4

Wash me clean

David knew he had done two great wrongs when he had arranged for Uriah to be killed, so that he could marry Uriah's wife, Bathsheba, who was already David's lover. With such a weight on his conscience, he could have given in to despair. But he did not. He threw himself on God's everlasting mercy, and prayed for forgiveness, and the strength to live a good life.

*Be gracious to me, O God, according to your
    loving kindness;
According to the greatness of your compassion blot out
    my transgressions.
Wash me thoroughly from my iniquity
And cleanse me from my sin.
For I know my transgressions,
And my sin is ever before me.
Behold, you desire truth in the innermost being,
And in the hidden part you will make me know wisdom.
Purify me with hyssop, and I shall be clean;
Wash me, and I shall be whiter than snow.
Make me to hear joy and gladness,
Let the bones which you have broken rejoice.
Hide your face from my sins
And blot out all my iniquities.
Create in me a clean heart, O God,
    And renew a steadfast spirit within me.
        Do not cast me away from your presence
            And do not take your Holy Spirit from me.
            Restore to me the joy of your salvation
            And sustain me with a willing spirit.
    The sacrifices of God are a broken spirit;
A broken and a contrite heart, O God,
You will not despise.*

Psalm 51:1–3, 6–12, 17

Forgiven

David knew the pain of a heavy conscience. He knew what he deserved, and what he had suffered. He also knew the joy that comes from confessing to God, and being forgiven.

Blessed is the one whose transgression is forgiven,
whose sin is covered.
Blessed is the man against whom the Lord counts
*   no iniquity,*
and in whose spirit there is no deceit.
For when I kept silent, my bones wasted away
through my groaning all day long.
For day and night your hand was heavy upon me;
my strength was dried up as by the heat of summer.
I acknowledged my sin to you,
and I did not cover my iniquity;
I said, 'I will confess my transgressions to the Lord,'
and you forgave the iniquity of my sin.

Therefore let everyone who is godly
offer prayer to you at a time when you may be found;
surely in the rush of great waters,
they shall not reach him.

You are a hiding place for me;
you preserve me from trouble;
you surround me with shouts of deliverance.
Psalm 32:1–7

Perfect

It may seem strange to modern ears to hear the law praised so enthusiastically. But perhaps we can learn that doing right can bring joy, health and strength. The law was drawn up by God, who knows what is best for us.

The Law of the Lord is perfect;
it gives us new life.
His teachings last forever,
and they give wisdom
to ordinary people.
The Lord's instruction is right;
it makes our hearts glad.
His commands shine brightly,
and they give us light.
Worshipping the Lord is sacred;
he will always be worshipped.

*They are worth more
than the finest gold
and are sweeter than honey
from a honeycomb.
By your teachings, Lord,
I am warned;
by obeying them,
I am greatly rewarded.
None of us know our faults.
Forgive me when I sin
without knowing it.
Let my words and my thoughts
be pleasing to you, Lord,
because you are my mighty rock and my protector.*
Psalm 19:7–12, 14

God Who Rescues

Keep me as the apple of your eye;
hide me in the shadow of your wings.
Psalm 17:8

How long?

Sometimes, hope and help can seem very far away. Our prayers seem to come back to us as an empty echo, as if God has forgotten us. But simply knowing that others have shared our isolation can sometimes help us feel less alone. And in time, we will know God's unfailing love again.

How long, O Lord? Will you forget me forever?
How long will you hide your face from me?
How long must I take counsel in my soul
and have sorrow in my heart all the day?

How long shall my enemy be exalted over me?
Consider and answer me, O Lord my God;
light up my eyes, lest I sleep the sleep of death,
lest my enemy say, 'I have prevailed over him,'
lest my foes rejoice because I am shaken.
But I have trusted in your steadfast love;
my heart shall rejoice in your salvation.
I will sing to the Lord,
because he has dealt bountifully with me.
Psalm 13

Your love is better than life

David wrote these words when he was in the desert, desperate for water. His longing for God was as powerful as his thirst. But, in his dry place, he chose to fill his mind with a powerful image of God's love and care in the past. This gave him the courage to look forwards, knowing God would fill him again.

O God, you are my God,
earnestly I seek you;
my soul thirsts for you,
my body longs for you,
in a dry and weary land
where there is no water.

I have seen you in the sanctuary
and beheld your power and your glory.
Because your love is better than life,
my lips will glorify you.
I will praise you as long as I live,
and in your name I will lift up my hands.
My soul will be satisfied as with the richest of foods;
with singing lips my mouth will praise you.
On my bed I remember you;
I think of you through the watches of the night.
Because you are my help,
I sing in the shadow of your wings.
My soul clings to you;
your right hand upholds me.
Psalm 63:1–8

More than watchmen for the morning

Prayers can rise up from the depths of our hearts, asking to be heard by God. And, although there is no immediate answer, we can learn to trust and wait. The image of a watchman waiting for the morning is a powerful one, conjuring up a picture of a lonely figure on a city wall, scanning the darkness for danger.

How the watchman must have longed for the safety of the day.

Out of the depths I have cried to You, O Lord.
Lord, hear my voice!
I wait for the Lord, my soul does wait,
And in his word do I hope.
My soul waits for the Lord
More than the watchmen for the morning;
Indeed, more than the watchmen for the morning.
Psalm 130:1–2, 5–6

I spread out my hands to you

There are times when it takes an act of courage to turn our thoughts to God and his goodness, and not to lose sight of his love. When there is nothing else to be done, we can still lean on God.

So my spirit grows faint within me;
my heart within me is dismayed.
I remember the days of long ago;
I meditate on all your works
and consider what your hands have done.
I spread out my hands to you;
my soul thirsts for you like a parched land.

Answer me quickly, O Lord;
my spirit faints with longing.
Do not hide your face from me
or I will be like those who go down to the pit.
Let the morning bring me word of your unfailing love,
for I have put my trust in you.
Show me the way I should go,
for to you I lift up my soul.
Psalm 143:4–8

God Who Knows Us

Be at rest once more, O my soul,
for the Lord has been good to you.
Psalm 116:7

You know me

There is real security in being known and loved by God completely. These words show a life that is mindful of God's loving, absolute involvement in every thought, word and action. They help us humbly to reflect that God knows our beginning and our end – and this knowledge is beyond our comprehension.

O Lord, you have searched me and known me!
You know when I sit down and when I rise up;
you discern my thoughts from afar.
You search out my path and my lying down
and are acquainted with all my ways.

Even before a word is on my tongue,
behold, O Lord, you know it altogether.
You hem me in, behind and before,
and lay your hand upon me.
Such knowledge is too wonderful for me;
it is high; I cannot attain it.
Where shall I go from your Spirit?
Or where shall I flee from your presence?
If I ascend to heaven, you are there!
If I make my bed in Sheol, you are there!
If I take the wings of the morning
and dwell in the uttermost parts of the sea,
even there your hand shall lead me,
and your right hand shall hold me.
If I say, 'Surely the darkness shall cover me,
and the light about me be night,'
even the darkness is not dark to you;
the night is bright as the day,
for darkness is as light with you.
For you formed my inward parts;
you knitted me together in my mother's womb.
I praise you, for I am fearfully and wonderfully made.
Wonderful are your works;
my soul knows it very well.
My frame was not hidden from you,
when I was being made in secret,

intricately woven in the depths of the earth.
Your eyes saw my unformed substance;
in your book were written, every one of them,
the days that were formed for me,
when as yet there were none of them.

Psalm 139:1–16

My soul is still

We can be restless, searching and anxious about many things. At such times, it is good to meditate on the psalm below. Its poignant gentleness reminds us that there will be questions without answers, and troubles we do not understand. But we can quieten our souls, and rest in the presence of a God who knows us and loves us absolutely.

> *My heart is not proud, O Lord,*
> *my eyes are not haughty;*
> *I do not concern myself with great matters*
> *or things too wonderful for me.*
> *But I have stilled and quieted my soul;*
> *like a weaned child with its mother,*
> *like a weaned child is my soul within me.*
> *O Israel, put your hope in the Lord*
> *both now and forevermore.*
> **Psalm 131**

Radiant!

'Those who look to him are radiant'; we read how good it is to know that when we call out to God, he hears us in this psalm, answering us with good things. Our response to such goodness is an active seeking to do good ourselves, and a vigorous and passionate wish for peace.

> *I sought the Lord, and he answered me*
> *and delivered me from all my fears.*
> *Those who look to him are radiant,*
> *and their faces shall never be ashamed.*
> *This poor man cried, and the Lord heard him*
> *and saved him out of all his troubles.*
> *The angel of the Lord encamps*
> *around those who fear him, and delivers them.*
> *Oh, taste and see that the Lord is good!*
> *Blessed is the man who takes refuge in him!*
> *Oh, fear the Lord, you his saints,*
> *for those who fear him have no lack!*
> *The young lions suffer want and hunger;*
> *but those who seek the Lord lack no good thing.*
> *Come, O children, listen to me;*
> *I will teach you the fear of the Lord.*
> *What man is there who desires life*
> *and loves many days, that he may see good?*
> *Keep your tongue from evil*
> *and your lips from speaking deceit.*
> *Turn away from evil and do good;*
> *seek peace and pursue it.*
> **Psalm 34:4–14**

God Who Heals and Strengthens

For you, O Lord, have delivered my soul from death,
my eyes from tears,
my feet from stumbling.
Psalm 116:8

The prayer of an afflicted man

At times when God seems far away, we can begin to pray by describing the pain that overwhelms us, using words such as the ones below. The psalms make good reading in the small hours, when we, and the owls, are sleepless.

I pray to you, Lord!
Please listen.
Don't hide from me
in my time of trouble.
Pay attention to my prayer
and quickly give an answer.
My days disappear like smoke,
and my bones are burning
as though in a furnace.
I am wasting away like grass,
and my appetite is gone.
My groaning never stops,
and my bones can be seen
through my skin.
I am like a lonely owl
in the desert
or a restless sparrow
alone on a roof.
Psalm 102:1–7

Darkness is my closest friend

There are times for asking God hard questions –
times when suffering and injustice are overwhelming
us. It is good to know that God will listen.

O Lord, the God who saves me,
day and night I cry out before you.
May my prayer come before you;
turn your ear to my cry.
For my soul is full of trouble
and my life draws near the grave.
I am counted among those who go down to the pit;
I am like a man without strength.
My eyes are dim with grief.
I call to you, O Lord, every day;
I spread out my hands to you.
But I cry to you for help, O Lord;
in the morning my prayer comes before you.
Why, O Lord, do you reject me
and hide your face from me?
You have taken my companions
and loved ones from me;
the darkness is my closest friend.
Psalm 88:1–4, 9, 13–14, 18

He turned his ear to me

In times of difficulty, it is worth reading the accounts of those who have come through pain and grief before. For God does hear the prayer of the anguished man, and he not only hears, but answers.

I love the Lord, for he heard my voice;
he heard my cry for mercy.
Because he turned his ear to me,
I will call on him as long as I live.
The cords of death entangled me,
the anguish of the grave came upon me;
I was overcome by trouble and sorrow.
Then I called on the name of the Lord:
'O Lord, save me!'
The Lord is gracious and righteous;
our God is full of compassion.
The Lord protects the simple-hearted;
when I was in great need, he saved me.
Be at rest once more, O my soul,
for the Lord has been good to you.
For you, O Lord, have delivered my soul from death,
my eyes from tears,
my feet from stumbling,
that I may walk before the Lord
in the land of the living.
Psalm 116:1–9

Prayer for one another

The psalms can also provide a model for prayer for those we know who are in trouble. These words could be used in such a way, replacing 'you' with a name. It is good to remember that God is to be trusted.

I pray that the Lord
will listen
when you
are in trouble,
and that the God of Jacob
will keep you safe.
May the Lord send help
from his temple
and come to your rescue
from Mount Zion.
May he remember your gifts
and be pleased
with what you bring.
May God do what you want most
and let all go well for you.
Psalm 20:1–4

God Worthy of Praise

*From the rising of the sun to the place where it sets,
the name of the Lord is to be praised.*
Psalm 113:3

Shout!

Many of the psalms were written for public worship.
They drew people into the Temple, united them in
their memories of God's help in the past, and gave
them strength and hope for the future. Joy is
contagious!

> *Shout joyfully to the Lord, all the earth.*
> *Serve the Lord with gladness;*
> *Come before him with joyful singing.*
> *Know that the Lord himself is God;*
> *It is he who has made us, and not we ourselves;*

We are his people and the sheep of his pasture.
Enter his gates with thanksgiving
And his courts with praise.
Give thanks to him, bless his name.
For the Lord is good;
His loving kindness is everlasting
And his faithfulness to all generations.
Psalm 100

Praise him

The praise of God is not limited to his people: in this
psalm below, the whole of creation is called to praise
in one extraordinary symphony of joy.

Praise the Lord!
Praise the Lord from the heavens;
praise him in the heights!
Praise him, all his angels;
praise him, all his hosts!
Praise him, sun and moon,
praise him, all you shining stars!
Praise him, you highest heavens,
and you waters above the heavens!
Let them praise the name of the Lord!
For he commanded and they were created.

And he established them forever and ever;
he gave a decree, and it shall not pass away.
Praise the Lord from the earth,
you great sea creatures and all deeps,
fire and hail, snow and mist,
stormy wind fulfilling his word!
Mountains and all hills,
fruit trees and all cedars!
Beasts and all livestock,
creeping things and flying birds!
Psalm 148:1–10

Speak of the glory of your kingdom

God's love and greatness is for all people, throughout
all ages. Praise has the power to lift the hearts and
faces of those who hear it, and remind them of God's
constant presence and power.

The Lord is gracious and merciful,
slow to anger and abounding in steadfast love.
The Lord is good to all,
and his mercy is over all that he has made.
All your works shall give thanks to you, O Lord,
and all your saints shall bless you!
They shall speak of the glory of your kingdom

and tell of your power,
to make known to the children of man your mighty deeds,
and the glorious splendour of your kingdom.
Your kingdom is an everlasting kingdom,
and your dominion endures throughout all generations.
Psalm 145:8–13

His love endures forever

Of all the things we have to be thankful for, the greatest is God's never-ending love. It is good to weave a recognition of that great love into any words we offer in thanks for all God's goodness.

Give thanks to the Lord, for he is good.
His love endures forever.
Give thanks to the God of gods.
His love endures forever.
Give thanks to the Lord of lords:
His love endures forever.
to him who alone does great wonders,
His love endures forever.
who by his understanding made the heavens,
His love endures forever.
who spread out the earth upon the waters,
His love endures forever.

who made the great lights –
His love endures forever.
the sun to govern the day,
His love endures forever.
the moon and stars to govern the night;
His love endures forever.
to the One who remembered us in our low estate
His love endures forever.
and freed us from our enemies,
His love endures forever.
and who gives food to every creature.
His love endures forever.
Give thanks to the God of heaven.
His love endures forever.
Psalm 136:1–9, 23–26